THIS NOTEBOOK BELONGS TO:

____